100 facts

Roman Britain

100 facts

Roman Britain

Philip Steele

Consultant: Jeremy Smith

Miles Kelly

First published in 2004 by Miles Kelly Publishing Ltd
Harding's Barn, Bardfield End Green, Thaxted, Essex, CM6 3PX

This edition printed in 2014

6 8 10 9 7

Publishing Director Belinda Gallagher
Creative Director Jo Cowan
Editorial Assistants Carly Blake
Volume Designer Michelle Cannatella
Proofreader Margaret Berrill
Indexer Jane Parker
Reprographics Liberty Newton, Ian Paulyn
Production Manager Elizabeth Collins
Assets Lorraine King

ISBN 978-1-84236-961-6

Printed in China

British Library Cataloguing-in-Publication Data
A catalogue record for this book is available from the British Library

ACKNOWLEDGEMENTS
The publishers would like to thank the following artists
who have contributed to this book:

Peter Dennis/Mike Foster/Richard Hook/John James/Janos Marffy
Alessandro Menchi/Andrea Morandi/Mike Saunders/Graham Sumner/Mike White

Cartoons by Mark Davis at Mackerel

Cover artwork by Graham Summer

www.mileskelly.net
info@mileskelly.net

Contents

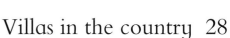

The Roman world

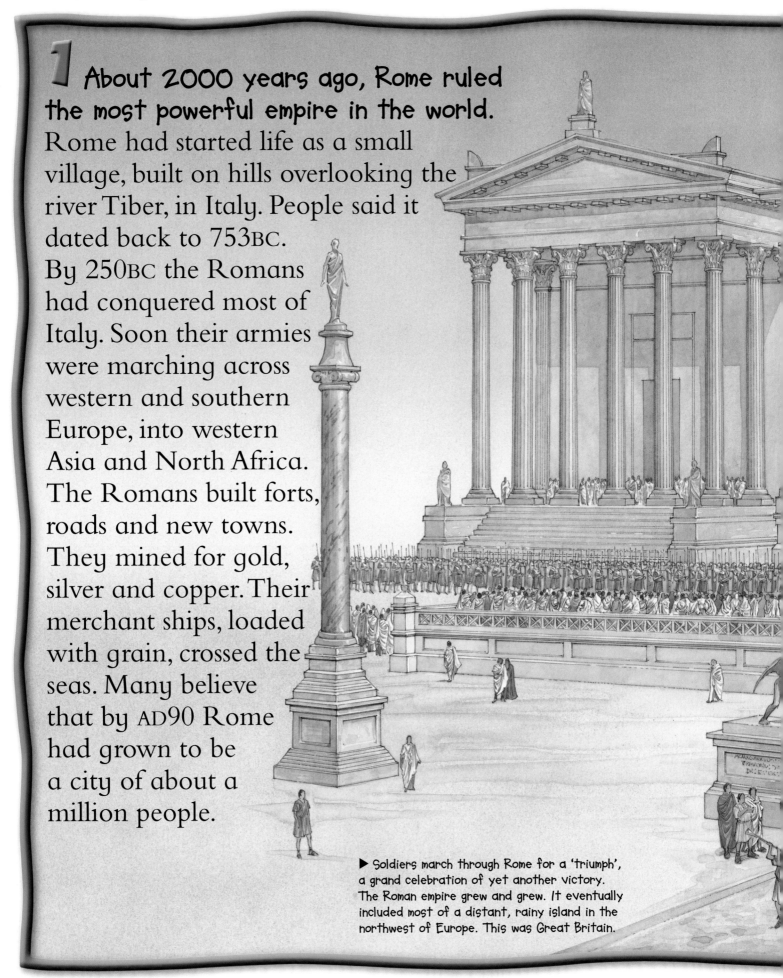

1 About 2000 years ago, Rome ruled the most powerful empire in the world. Rome had started life as a small village, built on hills overlooking the river Tiber, in Italy. People said it dated back to 753BC. By 250BC the Romans had conquered most of Italy. Soon their armies were marching across western and southern Europe, into western Asia and North Africa. The Romans built forts, roads and new towns. They mined for gold, silver and copper. Their merchant ships, loaded with grain, crossed the seas. Many believe that by AD90 Rome had grown to be a city of about a million people.

▶ Soldiers march through Rome for a 'triumph', a grand celebration of yet another victory. The Roman empire grew and grew. It eventually included most of a distant, rainy island in the northwest of Europe. This was Great Britain.

Enemies of Rome

2 **The people who lived in Great Britain in Roman times were called Britons.** Historians describe their way of life and the language they spoke as 'Celtic'. The Celtic family of peoples lived across large areas of Europe at this time, from Spain to Turkey. Other Celts included the Gaels of Ireland and the Gauls of France.

1 Votadini 2 Selgovae 3 Novantae 4 Brigantes
5 Parisi 6 Deceangli 7 Cornovii 8 Ordovices
9 Dobunni 10 Coritani 11 Iceni 12 Demetae
13 Trinovantes 14 Silures 15 Catuvellauni
16 Atrebates 17 Cantiaci 18 Durotriges 19 Dumnonii

▲ This map and key show British tribes and where they lived. Some southeastern tribes, like the Catuvellauni, had arrived from the mainland of Europe as recently as about 100BC. They were related to a tribe of Gauls called the Belgae.

MAKE A CELTIC MIRROR

You will need:

pencil scissors glue stick tin foil gold paint gold wrapping paper

1. Draw two circles onto card, a big one and a smaller one. Cut them out.

2. Draw the outline for the mirror handle onto card and cut it out. Glue one end to the big circle and the other end to the smaller circle (see below).

3. Paint both sides of the mirror with gold paint and allow to dry.

4. Cut out some tin foil the same size as the big circle and glue to one side of the circle.

5. Cut swirly shapes from gold wrapping paper. Glue them onto the back of your mirror as shown.

Front

Back

3 **The Britons belonged to many different tribes.** They were always fighting among themselves. Each tribe had its own king or queen and its own lands. There were important nobles, too, and priests and law-makers called druids. Most Britons were farmers and many were fine blacksmiths and iron-workers.

4 Most Britons lived in small settlements of large, round houses. These were made of timber and clay or stone, with thatched roofs. Some were built on hilltops, surrounded by fences and ditches for defence. Larger settlements or towns often surrounded royal halls.

▶ The Britons wove their clothes from linen and wool and wore cloaks fastened at the shoulder.

5 The Britons liked to wear gold jewellery. The Romans thought they were a bunch of show-offs, forever boasting about how brave they were. Women wore long dresses and the men wore tunics and trousers. No Roman man would have been seen dead in trousers!

▼ Celtic war chariots were made of wood, with iron-rimmed wheels. They carried warriors into battle.

6 Celtic warriors fought with long swords and spears and had horse-drawn chariots. In battle each warrior fought for himself. The Roman armies were very different. They were like a relentless fighting machine. Each soldier was drilled and trained to perfection.

Britons attacked

7 In August 55BC British warriors hurried to the cliffs near Dover as a Roman fleet approached with 10,000 soldiers on board. Their commander, Julius Caesar, wanted to punish the British tribes because they had been supporting the Gauls who were fighting against him. The Romans sailed along the coast and then waded ashore. After a few days of fighting, a storm blew up and damaged their ships. Caesar decided to play it safe and sail home.

I DON'T BELIEVE IT!

When ordered to invade Britain in AD43, the Roman troops downed weapons and went on strike. They complained that the order was unfair because the Channel shore marked the edge of the human world. Who knew what mysteries and monsters lay beyond?

◄ The first Roman into the water was the standard bearer of the Tenth Legion, or army group. The other troops leaped in and followed him to the shore.

8 **Caesar returned to Britain the following summer.** This time he took 800 ships, with 30,000 foot soldiers and 2000 cavalry. The troops fought their way through Kent and into Essex. At last they defeated the main alliance of tribes, which was led by Cassivellaunus, king of the Catuvellauni. Caesar made an alliance with a rival tribe called the Trinovantes and forced Cassivellaunus to pay tribute to Rome each year. Caesar left Britain after about ten weeks.

▲ The war fleet of 55BC was much bigger than the previous invasion. It included 28 warships like this one and hundreds of other ships to carry troops, horses, weapons, equipment and stores.

◀ These coins are marked 'Cunobelin'. They show the wealth of the Catuvellauni just before the Roman conquest.

9 **Julius Caesar became the most powerful man in Rome, but he was murdered in 44BC.** In the years that followed, the Romans found out more about Britain. They heard of rich prizes, such as tin mines and fields of golden wheat awaiting any invader. They sent merchants to spy out the land. They reported that the Catuvellauni were getting more powerful every day, under a new king called Cunobelinus.

10 **Cunobelinus died in about AD41.** Some rival British kingdoms called for the Romans to come and teach the pushy Catuvellauni a lesson. In AD42 the emperor Claudius put together a Roman army which was 40,000 strong. But its purpose was not just to attack one tribe. It aimed to bring the whole of Britain under Roman rule, once and for all.

Roman conquest

11 Roman troops, commanded by a general called Aulus Plautius, finally landed in Kent in the spring of AD43. They defeated Caratacus and Togodumnus, two sons of Cunobelinus. The biggest battle of all was probably fought by the river Medway, where the Romans broke through the massed tribes. Advancing into Essex, the Romans captured Camulodunum (Colchester), the new capital of the Catuvellauni. It was there that the emperor Claudius himself, on a fortnight's visit from Rome, took the surrender of 11 tribes.

Roman soldier

Celtic warrior

▲ Celtic warriors were strong fighters. Roman soldiers were not used to their fighting techniques. It would be many years before all of Britain was securely in Roman hands.

12 Some British rulers declared their support for the Romans straight away. Indeed, some of them had already made treaties with the Romans before AD44. Those rulers who backed the invaders did very nicely for themselves. Some were even given their own palaces, with every luxury Rome could afford. They drank good wine and had many slaves.

▶ The Romans sometimes used elephants to trample the enemy in battle. The emperor Claudius had some brought to Britain to impress the natives.

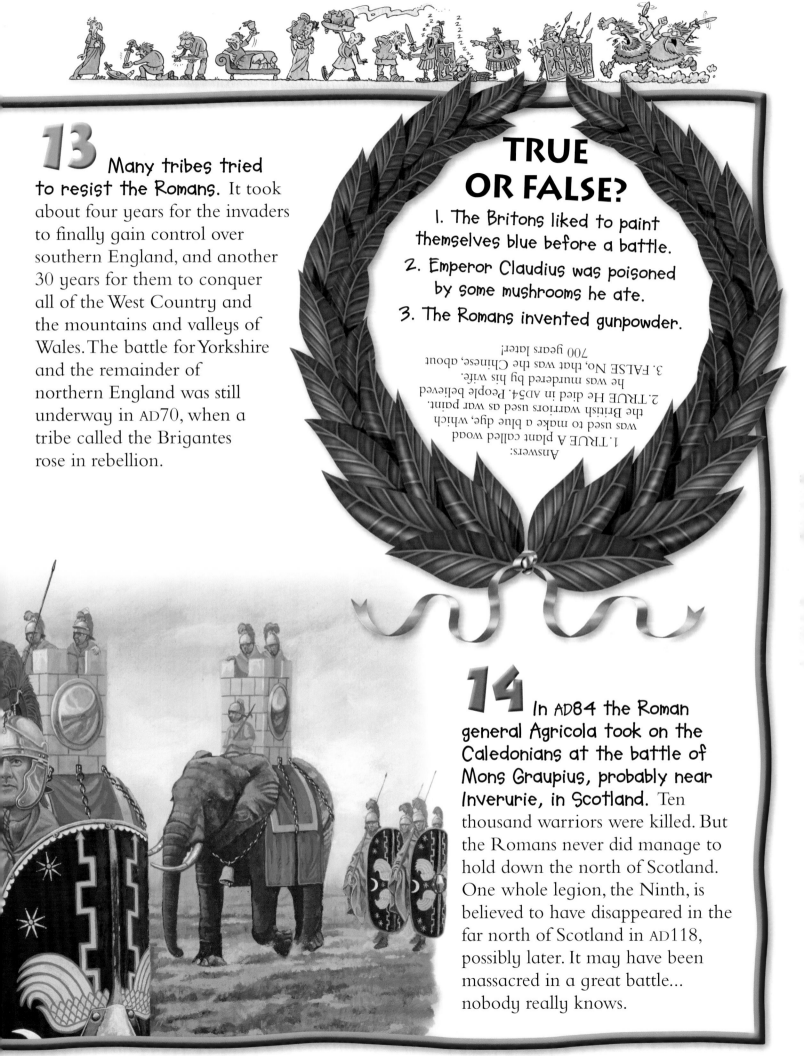

13 Many tribes tried to resist the Romans. It took about four years for the invaders to finally gain control over southern England, and another 30 years for them to conquer all of the West Country and the mountains and valleys of Wales. The battle for Yorkshire and the remainder of northern England was still underway in AD70, when a tribe called the Brigantes rose in rebellion.

TRUE OR FALSE?

1. The Britons liked to paint themselves blue before a battle.
2. Emperor Claudius was poisoned by some mushrooms he ate.
3. The Romans invented gunpowder.

Answers:
1. TRUE A plant called woad was used to make a blue dye, which the British warriors used as war paint.
2. TRUE He died in AD54. People believed he was murdered by his wife.
3. FALSE No, that was the Chinese, about 700 years later!

14 In AD84 the Roman general Agricola took on the Caledonians at the battle of Mons Graupius, probably near Inverurie, in Scotland. Ten thousand warriors were killed. But the Romans never did manage to hold down the north of Scotland. One whole legion, the Ninth, is believed to have disappeared in the far north of Scotland in AD118, possibly later. It may have been massacred in a great battle... nobody really knows.

Rebels in chains

15 In their first summer in Britain, the Romans made a big mistake. They let Caratacus escape. Caratacus was the son of Cunobelinus, and a cunning fighter. He and his followers joined up with tribes in Wales. From there, they launched many attacks on the Romans. Defeated at last in AD51, Caratacus fled to the territory of the Brigantes. Their queen, Cartimandua, handed him over to the Romans. She had agreed to keep the peace with them and did not want any more trouble.

▲ After his betrayal, Caratacus and his family were taken to Rome to be paraded as prisoners of war. However, he made such a strong speech in his own defence, that the emperor Claudius pardoned him.

▶ Boudicca's advance was finally checked in a terrible battle. About 80,000 British warriors may have been killed and Boudicca committed suicide.

16
In AD60 the Romans launched an attack on the druids (Celtic priests) because they were believed to be harbouring rebels. In AD60 the Romans stormed the druids' sacred island of Mona (Anglesey, in North Wales). As the troops crossed the water, women screamed, warriors hurled spears and the druids called down curses. All were slaughtered by the Romans.

17
Suddenly, the Romans called off their attack on Mona and hurried away. Messengers had brought terrible news. The Iceni of East Anglia were in revolt. Their king, Prasutagus, had already made a treaty with the Romans. But when he died, Roman troops had seized his lands and assaulted his family. His wife, Boudicca, was enraged. She summoned the tribes to war. They burned down Camulodunum, Londinium (London) and Verulamium (St Albans), killing all who lived there.

I DON'T BELIEVE IT!
While the Iceni rebels were sweeping through the southeast, Roman troops had to march back from North Wales at high speed. They covered 400 kilometres in just 14 days – and faced new battles when they got there. The cavalry raced ahead of them.

Britannia!

18 Britain was now 'Britannia', a province of the mighty Roman empire, with its capital at Londinium. It was ruled by a governor. The province was divided into territories, military settlements and towns. Each had a council and elected magistrates to enforce the law.

◀ This coin from AD150 shows the figure of a woman with a spear and shield as an emblem of Britannia.

19 The Roman army kept strict control over Britannia. They set up military camps during the conquest, and soon replaced their leather tents with strong forts built of timber and then of stone. These could cover 20 hectares of land. They had barracks, officers' headquarters, parade grounds, grain stores, workshops, hospitals, baths and toilets, too. Often a village or a town would grow up outside the walls of the fort as well.

▲ Roman forts were built and repaired by the troops themselves. The everyday work of a soldier involved carpentry, construction and engineering as much as fighting battles.

▲ Ruins like this help us understand how the Britons lived under Roman rule. The site in Wales has the remains of stone huts, grain stores and walls. It probably belonged to a local chieftain.

PLACE NAME DETECTIVE

The Roman word for a camp or a fort was CASTRUM. Any places in modern Britain ending –CASTER or –CHESTER were probably once military centres of the Roman occupation. Can you think of any near you? If not, check any road map of Britain.

20 **During the conquest, many Britons had been killed in battle or enslaved.** But as the years went by, more and more Britons in the towns took on Roman customs. Even so, in more remote countryside the old Celtic way of life continued much the same as before, hunting, herding cattle or sowing crops.

▼ A travelling merchant shows jewellery to a wealthy Roman lady. She needs a new necklace for the governor's dinner party.

21 **Soon there were quite a few Romans living in Britannia.** There were young officers newly arrived from Rome, upper-class ladies, children, doctors, shopkeepers and servants. Many Roman soldiers settled in British towns when they left the army, sometimes taking a local wife. Not all the newcomers came from Italy. Soldiers, merchants and slaves arrived from all over the Roman empire – including Germany, Greece, Spain and North Africa.

Marching with the Eagles

22 **The Roman army was divided into legions, each of about 3000 to 5000 men.** The legions were moved around the empire as needed. Each had its own battle standards, tall poles topped with an emblem such as an aquila – an eagle of gold. Legions were divided into smaller groups called cohorts and centuries. Other army groups called auxiliaries provided support. These were made up of troops who were not Roman citizens.

23 **A soldier in a legion was expected to serve for 25 years.** Each new recruit was given long hours of marching, weapons-training and drilling. On active service he had to carry his own weapons, armour, tools and rations such as hard biscuits, cheese and sour wine.

24 **A legionary in the early days of the conquest wore a helmet of iron or bronze with cheek guards and a flap to protect the neck.** Caesar's troops wore shirts of iron mail, but by the AD100s, armour made of metal plates was being strapped over the soldier's tunic. A new type of shield was being carried by then, too. It was rectangular and curved and made from wood and leather.

25 The legionary was armed with a javelin and a short sword. Cavalry carried a longer sword. Slings and a variety of spears or daggers were also used in battle. Auxiliaries from Asia were often used as archers, armed with bows and arrows.

26 When they stormed a Celtic hill fort, Roman troops would often form a 'tortoise'. This formation was created by soldiers lifting their shields above their heads. Spears and rocks would bounce off the tortoise's 'shell'.

QUIZ

1. When were Roman soldiers allowed to marry?
a. Any time b. After 10 years' service c. On retirement
2. Who first used saddles on horses?
a. Celts b. Romans c. Germans
3. How long was a Roman soldier expected to serve?
a. 5 years b. 15 years
c. 25 years

Answers:
1C 2A 3C

◀ Marching with the legions was exhausting. Troops were expected to cover about 30 kilometres a day – and after that, dig their defences for the night.

27 Giant catapults were used to hurl arrows or pointed missiles called bolts at the enemy. Round stones and heavy boulders were hurled by a machine called a ballista. The strong timber gates of a hillfort could be destroyed by a battering ram or by fire, as happened in AD43 at Maiden Castle in Dorset.

Frontier defence

28 Great Britain formed the northwestern frontier of the Roman empire. The Romans never conquered Ireland, so most of the frontier followed the coastline. In the north of Britain, however, it crossed the land, and was defended by a wall.

▲ Hadrian's Wall became the permanent frontier. From Bowness in the west and Wallsend in the east, there were 15 larger forts.

29 The emperor Hadrian gave his name to the great northern wall, which was begun in AD122. It ran for 117 kilometres, from the Solway Firth to the river Tyne. Its aim was to keep out the tribes on the northern side and to prevent them from making alliances with tribes on the southern side. The wall made it easier to move troops and supplies.

▶ A Roman patrol brings in two Picts ('painted people') from beyond the wall, for questioning.

30 Hadrian's Wall was built of stone, about 4 metres high by 3 metres wide. It was defended by ditches and at every Roman mile (1500 metres) there was a mini-fort with a tower to guard crossing points. There was a string of larger forts along the wall, and the large Vindolanda base (Chesterholm) was built on an east-west road to the south of the wall.

31 Serving on Hadrian's Wall must have been boring for the auxiliary soldiers – Romans, Gauls, Dutch, Germans and other defenders of the empire. When the troops weren't building and digging, they had marches, weapons-training or drill on the parade ground. In their spare time they hunted, gambled, drank wine or beer, or wrote letters home. Many documents have survived, such as accounts books, requests for leave, even a birthday invitation from an officer's wife to her friend.

32 Twenty years after Hadrian's Wall was started, the Romans built another wall across the Scottish Lowlands, between the Firth of Forth and the river Clyde. The Antonine Wall was a great bank of soil built over cobble stones. It never became a permanent frontier.

33 Coastal defences were built in places where there was risk of attack. Saxon raiders from mainland Europe crossed the North Sea and the Channel. From about AD280 onwards, eastern and southern coasts, known as the 'Saxon shore', were defended by castle-like forts and stone walls.

A network of roads

34 **The Romans introduced the first planned system of roads in Britain.** Some were minor routes but others were up to 12 metres wide, straight and well-drained. The chief aim of these roads was to allow the legions to march quickly from one part of the country to another. No better roads were built until the 1800s.

▶ Stone pillars (milestones) were erected to show distances between towns in Roman miles. Many of them showed which emperor was ruling at the time. This milestone bears the name Victorinus, who came to power in AD269.

35 **Roads were made using whichever stone was available locally.** The route was carefully surveyed and forest was cleared well back from the verges, to prevent ambush. Layers of broken flint and crushed stone were laid as foundations. The surface was generally of gravel, but sometimes paved. The roads were built by the army using troops or slaves as labour.

◀ A Roman surveyor checks how level a new road is while slaves carry baskets of flint and gravel.

36 The Roman road network was centred upon Londinium (London). From there, main roads went out to the chief army towns – Dubris (Dover), Camulodunum (Colchester), Noviomagus (Chichester), Isca Dumnoniorum (Exeter), Viroconium (Wroxeter) and Eboracum (York). A cross-country route from Exeter to Lindum (Lincoln) marked the temporary frontier of the advancing Romans in AD47. Some sections of these routes still carry traffic today.

QUIZ

1. How far could a Roman soldier march in one day?
a. 10 kilometres b. 20 kilometres c. 50 kilometres

2. How many kilometres of road did the Romans build in Britannia?
a. 900 b. 4000 c. 9000

3. Who repaired roads and bridges? a. local councils b. slaves c. local farmers

Answers:
1C 2C 3A

37 The most important travellers on the roads were the official messengers, who rode on horseback. They travelled at speed, obtaining fresh horses from wayside inns. Some travellers used fast, lightweight carts pulled by mules, while others rode in slower, horse-drawn carriages. Heavy goods were carried in wooden wagons hauled by teams of oxen.

▼ Slow traffic would move onto the broad verges to let a courier or cavalry unit ride down the central roadway at speed.

Ox-cart

Mule cart

Official courier on horseback

Roman towns

38 The Romans built towns, often on the sites of the former tribal capitals of the Britons. Smaller towns and villages grew up around crossroads, along rivers and by the sea. The Romans who moved into these towns were officials, lawyers, traders or craftworkers. They were soon joined by those Britons who could afford to take up the Roman way of life.

39 The Roman period saw the first proper towns in Britain. They had paved streets with houses laid out according to a grid plan, market places, temples, statues, public baths, shops and workshops. Major towns or cities were surrounded by defensive walls.

40 Londinium (London) was sited on the banks of the river Thames. It was ideally sited for trade with the rest of the empire. A long, wooden bridge was built across the river. London became a great centre of trade and was the biggest city in the province. At its peak it had a population of about 45,000. An army fort was built, a huge town hall, or basilica, a market place or forum and temples.

41 Townhouses were built of timber, and later stone and brick. Shopkeepers and craftworkers mostly lived on the premises behind their shopfronts. Some houses had six or more rooms and were quite grand, with painted walls, tiled floors, courtyards and gardens.

42 The Romans were great engineers. Their towns were supplied with fresh water by aqueducts (water channels) and pipes made of lead and timber. Towns had drains and sewers.

▲ The biggest towns in Britannia, such as Londinium, served as military bases.

25

43 **The Romans believed in many gods and goddesses.** There was all-powerful Jupiter, Venus the goddess of love, Mercury the messenger of the gods, Diana the goddess of hunting and Saturn the god of farming. Every Roman knew old stories about the gods. In these, the gods behaved very much like humans, quarrelling and falling in love.

▲ A statue of Jupiter, king of the Roman gods. Images of the gods were placed in temples and public places.

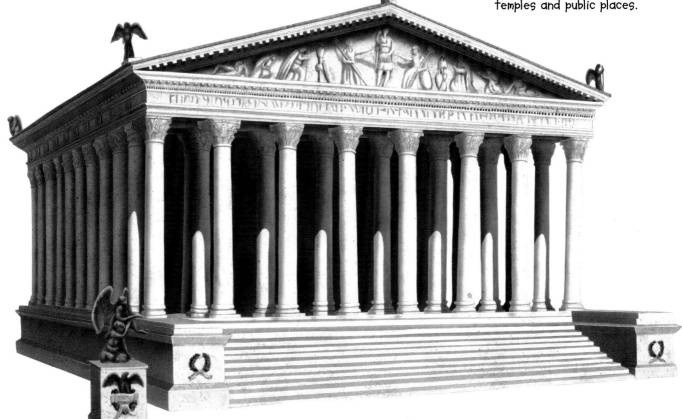

44 **Some Roman temples were built in stone, often with splendid pillars and painted walls.** At the centre was a sanctuary or shrine. People might make offerings or give thanks to the gods, but there was no public worship.

▲ The great temple of Claudius at Colchester was one of the first in Britannia. It was built to impress the Britons, but was destroyed by Boudicca. It had to be rebuilt after her rebellion was crushed.

45 **Some Roman emperors were officially worshipped as gods.** It helped them keep control over the people, if they could claim to be super-human. A great temple to the emperor Claudius was built at Colchester. He was a lame, stammering man, who was very clever. He must have smiled to himself at the thought of being honoured as a god.

TRUE OR FALSE?

1. January is named after Janus, the Roman god of doorways.
2. The Romans made human sacrifices to their gods.
3. Many of the planets are named after Roman gods.

Answers:
1. TRUE Janus was shown with two faces, one looking backwards and one looking forwards. 2. FALSE Animals were sacrificed to some of the gods. 3 TRUE We have named all the planets except Earth after Roman gods and goddesses.

▲ Mithras, the Persian god of light, was often shown slaying a bull.

46 **All sorts of foreign religions became popular in Britannia over the years.** Isis was an ancient Egyptian goddess who gained many followers. Mithras, the Persian god of light, was very popular with the troops. Many temples were built to honour Mithras, including one in London.

▼ This statue honours a tribal goddess called Brigantia, who was reckoned to be the same as the Roman goddess of wisdom, Minerva.

47 **In the countryside, the Britons still worshipped the old Celtic gods and goddesses.** Many of the Roman newcomers happily adopted these gods, too. They identified them with similar Roman gods and built temples and local shrines to a lot of them.

Villas in the country

48 **Villas were large Roman country houses.** They were normally built at the centre of a large estate, with orchards and fields of wheat, flocks of sheep or herds of cattle. Labour was provided by slaves. Villa owners were often the wealthier Romans, such as government officials or retired army officers. Many Britons also became landowners in the Roman style.

49 **Over the years, villa design became more and more luxurious.** The buildings had dining rooms, kitchens, bedrooms, bathrooms and courtyards. They even had central heating. Warm air from a furnace passed along channels under the floor and then up a flue behind the walls.

▼ Country villas were owned mainly by the rich. The first villas were simple farmhouses but as Rome prospered, villas became magnificent mansions built all over the empire. Walls were covered with paintings and beautiful mosaics decorated the floors.

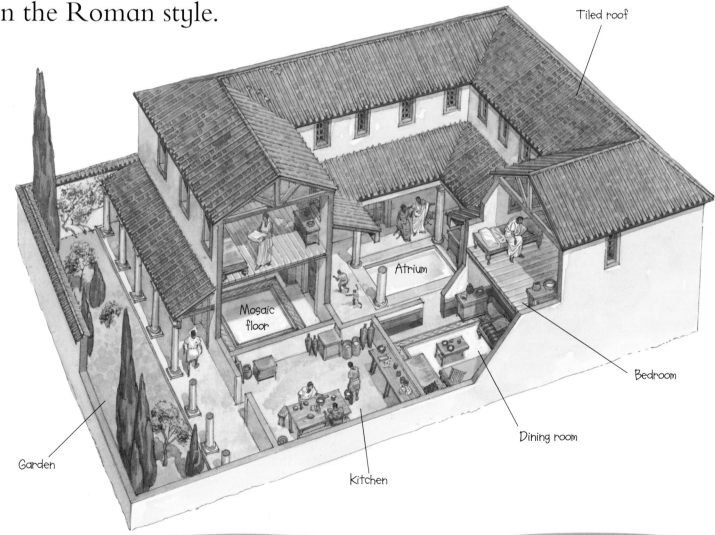

Tiled roof

Atrium

Mosaic floor

Bedroom

Dining room

Garden

Kitchen

50

Floors were decorated with mosaics.

Mosaics are pictures built up from thousands of small tiles made from coloured stone or pottery, set in cement. Some mosaics featured patterns, others showed images of gods, seasons, animals or fruit. Craftsmen would travel from one site to another to lay new floors.

▲ This mosaic may have been designed for the floor of a bathhouse.

MAKE A ROMAN MOSAIC

You will need:

card   pencil
coloured paper   glue

1. Take an A3-size sheet of card.

2. Draw the outlines of your picture or pattern.

3. Cut or tear paper of various colours into fragments about one centimetre square.

4. Glue them to the card, building up the picture within the outlines you have drawn.

51

Houses and gardens were often decorated with statues.

Stone carvers also produced shrines to the gods who were believed to protect the household from harm.

52

The estates also offered hunting with dogs.

Deer were a popular choice of prey as venison was a welcome addition to the menu at dinner time. Boar (wild pig) was common in Britain and was a fierce animal when cornered by hunters with nets and spears.

▶ A charging boar could send a hunter flying and its sharp tusks could gash a leg badly.

Working the land

53 The estates of the new villas might cover an area of 500 to 1000 hectares. They were often sited on the best farmland. Farming methods began to improve. The Romans dug new wells. They raised cattle, sheep, pigs, goats, ducks and geese and improved them by breeding from the best stock. They built new ovens for drying grain before threshing, a useful invention in Britain's damp climate.

▲ Fruit trees were planted around many Roman villas in Britain and were carefully tended through the seasons.

◄ Pairs of oxen were used for ploughing or hauling the heavy wooden farm wagons.

54 New farm tools came into use on Roman estates. Long scythes were used for cutting hay, instead of short-bladed sickles. The Roman plough was heavier and cut through the soil more easily.

Turnip

Parsnip

Carrot

55

The Romans brought crops that had been unknown to the Britons. They grew rye, oats and new root and leaf crops such as cabbages, carrots, parsnips and turnips. Roman estate managers planted the first plum and walnut trees and they tried growing grape vines in the more sheltered, southern regions of Britain.

◀ Vegetables grown in Roman Britain included carrots, turnips and parsnips.

56

Retired Roman soldiers who settled in Britannia used to grow vegetables on small plots by their home. They might keep ducks on the pond or pottery hives full of busy bees. Bees were valued very highly, for honey was the only food sweetener in the days before sugar was used.

57

Large areas of Britain were still farmed by Britons who had not adopted Roman ways. These smaller farms surrounded traditional thatched dwellings, often in the more remote, highland areas of Britain. The farmers herded sheep and cattle and grew barley and a type of wheat called spelt.

TRUE OR FALSE?

1. The Romans built ovens for drying grain before threshing.
2. Cattle were used for ploughing.
3. The Romans planted the first plum trees.

Answers:
1. TRUE This was a useful Roman invention. 2. FALSE Oxen were used for ploughing. 3. TRUE The Romans planted the first plum and walnut trees.

Fair trade

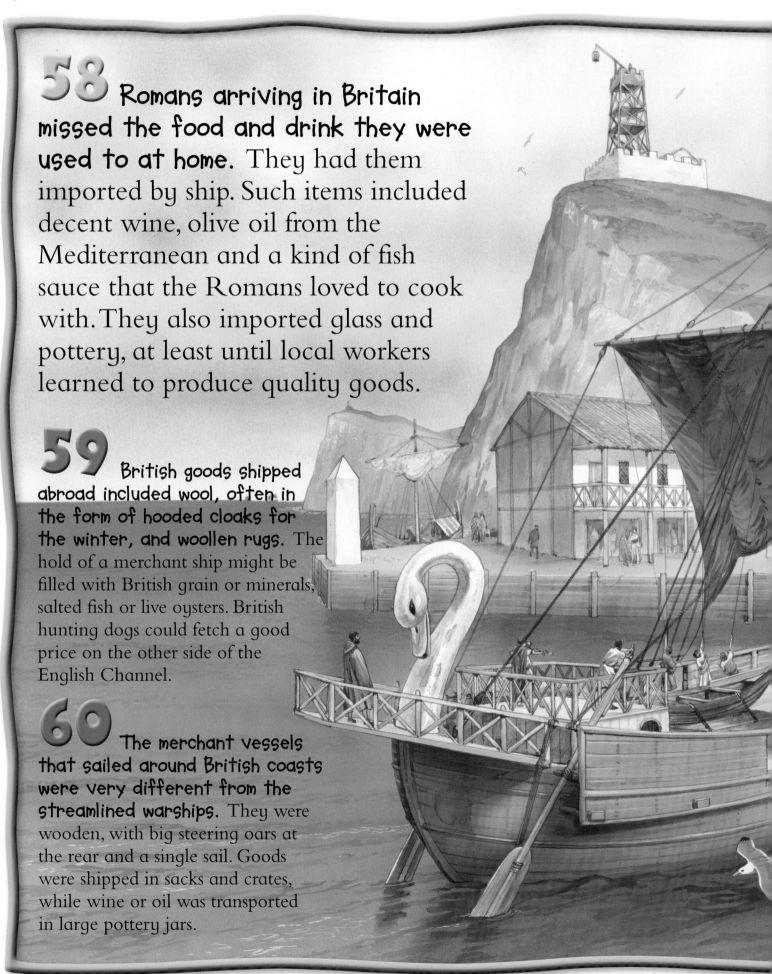

58 **Romans arriving in Britain missed the food and drink they were used to at home.** They had them imported by ship. Such items included decent wine, olive oil from the Mediterranean and a kind of fish sauce that the Romans loved to cook with. They also imported glass and pottery, at least until local workers learned to produce quality goods.

59 **British goods shipped abroad included wool, often in the form of hooded cloaks for the winter, and woollen rugs.** The hold of a merchant ship might be filled with British grain or minerals, salted fish or live oysters. British hunting dogs could fetch a good price on the other side of the English Channel.

60 **The merchant vessels that sailed around British coasts were very different from the streamlined warships.** They were wooden, with big steering oars at the rear and a single sail. Goods were shipped in sacks and crates, while wine or oil was transported in large pottery jars.

61 River banks and ports had wharves of timber or stone. Some harbours had their own lighthouses, a blazing beacon on top of a tall tower.

▼ Goods were often transported by boat as it was often easier and cheaper than by road. The Romans had a huge fleet of ships carrying goods to and from all parts of the empire.

I DON'T BELIEVE IT!
Roman ships have been found preserved in the mud of the river Thames. Archaeologists have also discovered London's first wharves, along with dockers' tools and pottery jars.

62 A single coinage was used across the whole Roman empire. It was made up of the gold aureus, the silver denarius and the brass sestertius. In the 300s, a mint was set up in London to make coins.

63 The business centre of a Roman town was the forum. When shops opened for business, people could buy everything from lamps and tools to pots and pans. Officials watched weights and measures closely and cheating market traders were punished.

A hard day's work

64 The Britons had made good pottery long before the arrival of the Romans. However, under Roman rule, pottery-making became a big industry. The design of the kilns in which pottery was fired and hardened was improved. Dishes, jugs and kitchenware were turned out on a large scale. Many showing the maker's trademark have survived.

▲ Potteries grew up wherever there was good clay, many in Oxfordshire and southern England. The town of Durovernum Cantiacorum (Canterbury, in Kent) was a centre of glass-making.

65 Weaving, too, became a big industry under the Romans. Work was usually done by poorer women. The wool was still spun into yarn at home, using a hand-held spindle. The weaving and finishing of the cloth was now often carried out in larger workshops, or mills.

▼ The Romans had no spinning wheels. Instead, a spindle such as this was twirled around. It stretched and twisted the woollen fibre into yarn for weaving.

66 The Romans hoped that Britain's minerals would make them rich. The miners were mostly slaves and led wretched lives. They mined for gold and copper in Wales, tin in Cornwall, coal in the northeast, iron in the southeast and Midlands, lead in the West Country and Derbyshire. They could get silver from the lead by heating it to a very high temperature.

67 The Romans could teach the Celts little about ironworking and blacksmithing. That was their speciality. Business boomed and there were always red-hot axes, pans or horseshoes to be beaten out with the hammer.

▲ The forge was at the centre of every village and town. More and more iron goods were being made and repaired in Roman times.

QUIZ
Can you give each Roman or British worker the right tool for the job?

1. Stonemason
2. Sailor
3. Potter
4. Blacksmith
5. Weaver

a. Anchor
b. Loom
c. Wheel
d. Chisel
e. Anvil

Answers:
1d 2a 3c 4e 5b

68 As the Romans settled in Britannia, they needed stone to build new towns, bridges, aqueducts and temples. Quarries were worked all over the country. Rock was heated with fire until it cracked, then levered away in slabs and cut into blocks.

Learning and medicine

69 **The children of wealthier Britons and Romans living in towns went to school at age six to seven.** Here they would learn reading, writing, history, sports and arithmetic. Most children left school at about the age of 11 and might have continued with their education at home.

71 **The Romans had various ways of writing.** They could scratch letters onto a wooden tablet covered in wax, using a sharp point called a stylus. Important documents were written with pen and ink on parchment (prepared animal hide) or papyrus (a type of paper made from reeds). School children practised writing on broken pottery.

◄ A tutor teaches his pupils how to recognize the letters on a scroll of parchment. Lessons tended to be dull and tutors often hit the children if they got the answers wrong.

70 **Girls might be expected to learn weaving and some were given lessons in playing an instrument called the lyre.** Girls from important families might be taught the same lessons as the boys. All girls were expected to learn how to run a household, as a training for married life.

72
Arithmetic for beginners involved much counting with the fingers of both hands. Instead of calculators, Roman children used a counting frame, or abacus. They pushed counters along the rows to work out sums.

Abacus

▼ Roman surgeons used many instruments for operations.

Spoons were used for giving medicine

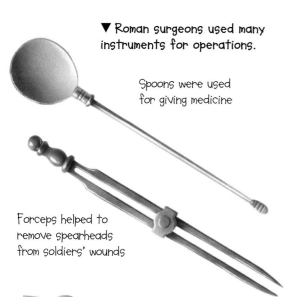

Forceps helped to remove spearheads from soldiers' wounds

73
The Britons in the countryside spoke a Celtic language known as Brythonic. This later developed into the Welsh, Breton and Cornish languages. The Romans in the towns spoke Latin, and soon any Briton who wanted to get on in life had to learn it too. Latin remained the language of the Church, the law and universities long after Roman rule of Britain had come to an end.

74
Science and medicine were still quite basic and few people lived to see old age. There were many herbal medicines and potions and some of these did work. Doctors dealt with eye infections and surgeons carried out all sorts of operations. Poppy juice and wine were used as anaesthetics (pain relievers).

Hooks held wounds open during operations

Ointment was applied with a spatula

Let's speak LATIN!
Here are some of the Latin words that the Britons had to learn.

boy ....puer   (POO-er)
girl...................puella   (poo-ELL-a)
British..............Britannicus   (brit-ANN-i-coos)
soldier..............miles   (MEE-lays)
sea ....mare   (MAH-ray)
island...............insula   (IN-soo-lah)
horse................equus   (ec-WUSS)

Time to relax

75 Every Roman town had to have its public baths. Even the better-off British enjoyed bathing too, while the job of the slaves was to stoke the furnace that heated the water. The bath house was the noisiest building in town, echoing with the sound of splashing water and chatter. Men and women bathed separately. They went there to get clean, to relax, to have a massage or a work-out or to gossip with friends. One of the most popular Roman baths was at Aquae Sulis (Bath).

I DON'T BELIEVE IT!

Chariot-racers had the same following of fans as the football stars of today. Everyone knew their names and nicknames and followed their favourite team, such as the reds or the greens.

76 At Isca Silurum (Caerleon, in South Wales) crowds watched gladiators fight. Gladiators were slaves or prisoners who were given a chance to win popularity or freedom in public combat. They often fought to the death. Other entertainments included boxing and chariot-racing. Amphitheatres in Britannia were not as grand as those in Rome.

77 Any fair-sized town had its own open-air theatre. Rows of wooden seats, set into a bank of earth, rose in a half circle around the stage. The show might include dancing, music, plays about Roman gods and goddesses, and comic sketches. Groups of actors probably toured Britannia, travelling from one town to another.

▼ The baths at Aquae Sulis (Bath) had changing rooms and lockers, hot baths, warm baths and cold baths – but no soap. Bathers oiled their bodies and then scraped themselves clean.

79 Children's toys included marbles, dolls and toy chariots. Roman and British children must have swum in the rivers in summer, raced each other round the houses and played different ball games.

78 The Romans loved playing games and gambling. The clatter of rolling dice could be heard in bath houses, inns and barrack rooms around Britannia. Favourite games were called 'Tables', 'Robbers' and 'Three Stones' (which was a version of noughts-and-crosses). A popular girls' game was tossing little bones into the air and seeing how many they could catch on the back of the hand.

▼ Boards made of pottery and little gaming pieces of bone, glass, clay or ivory have have been dug up at Londinium (London) and Calleva Atrebatum (Silchester).

39

Togas and jewels

80 The most common Roman dress was a simple, practical tunic, which was worn by working people, slaves and children. A woollen cloak was worn for warmth. Important men wore a white robe called a toga. It looked good, but it was bulky and uncomfortable to wear. Men of high rank wore togas with a purple trim.

▼ ▶ Roman ladies wore fine jewellery, some of it made locally.

Gold earrings

Jet bangle

Gold ring

81 Most boys and girls wore togas like their parents. Married women wore a coloured dress called a stola and a shawl called a palla, which could be draped over the head and shoulders.

▼ At the height of the empire, women wore a brightly coloured robe called a stola and a shawl known as palla. Children wore knee-length tunics. Men too, took an interest in fashion, and wealthy families wore only the finest cloths.

82 Like today, hairstyles went in and out of fashion. At the time Hadrian's Wall was being built, Roman men were cleanshaven. Later it was fashionable for them to grow beards. Women would curl, plait or pin up their hair. Wigs and hair extensions were popular, as were headdresses and hairbands. Make-up included lipstick, eyeshadow and a white face powder made from chalk or even poisonous lead. Perfumes and scented oils were kept in beautiful little bottles and jars.

85 Working clothes included wrappings of cloth worn as leggings and hoods to keep out the cold. Leather cloaks were waterproof against the British rain.

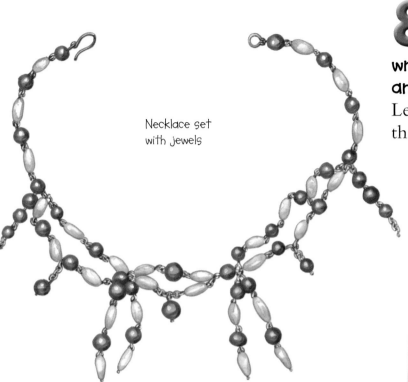

Necklace set with jewels

83 Men and women wore rings of gold, silver or bronze. Many of these were set with amber or precious stones. Rich women wore necklaces and earrings of gold and pearls, while poorer women made do with beads of glass or ceramics. In Yorkshire the shiny black stone known as jet (a sort of fossilized wood) was carved into bangles and beads. Cloaks were fastened with fine brooches.

84 Romans wore leather sandals on their feet. Even soldiers wore these, with studded soles so that they were not worn out by marching. Leather shoes, too, have been found in London. Boots were worn for riding or for muddy, winter days.

MAKE A ROMAN PENDANT

You will need:
scissors thread or wool card
paint paintbrush

1. For the chain, cut the thread or wool to the right length for your own neck.

2. For the pendant, cut out a disc of card.

3. Paint a design on the card. It could be a dolphin or perhaps a scary monster called a gorgon, with a woman's face but tangled hair full of snakes.

4. Make a hole near the top of the disc and thread the 'chain' through it.

Eat, drink and be merry!

86 Roman kitchens included ovens for baking bread, raised brick hearths for boiling and simmering and spits for roasting. Oil and other foods were stored in large pottery jars. Hung up in the kitchen you might find a hare or a duck and spread out on the tables would be herbs, spices and vegetables.

87 The Romans did not start the day with a big breakfast, just bread and fruit, if they ate it at all. Lunch might be a light meal of leftovers from the night before. Many people in towns would buy a quick snack from a stall on the street, perhaps a hot meat pie, a sausage or a sweet pastry. The main meal, *cena* ('kay-nah'), was eaten in the evening. It might include three courses with meat or fish, vegetables and fruit.

88 A Roman banquet was a special event. The guests would eat lying on couches around a low table. A dining room with three couches was called a *triclinium*. Servants would bring in up to seven or eight courses. There would be starters, salads, dumplings, omelettes and shellfish. Main dishes might include kidneys, liver, roast venison in plum sauce or young goat cooked in cream.

▼ Food was cooked in pots and pans made of iron, bronze or pottery. Meals were prepared by slaves.

Charcoal was burned in the stove

89 Out in the countryside, British farmers sat down to much more basic meals. They might eat hare or fish, barley cakes or broth.

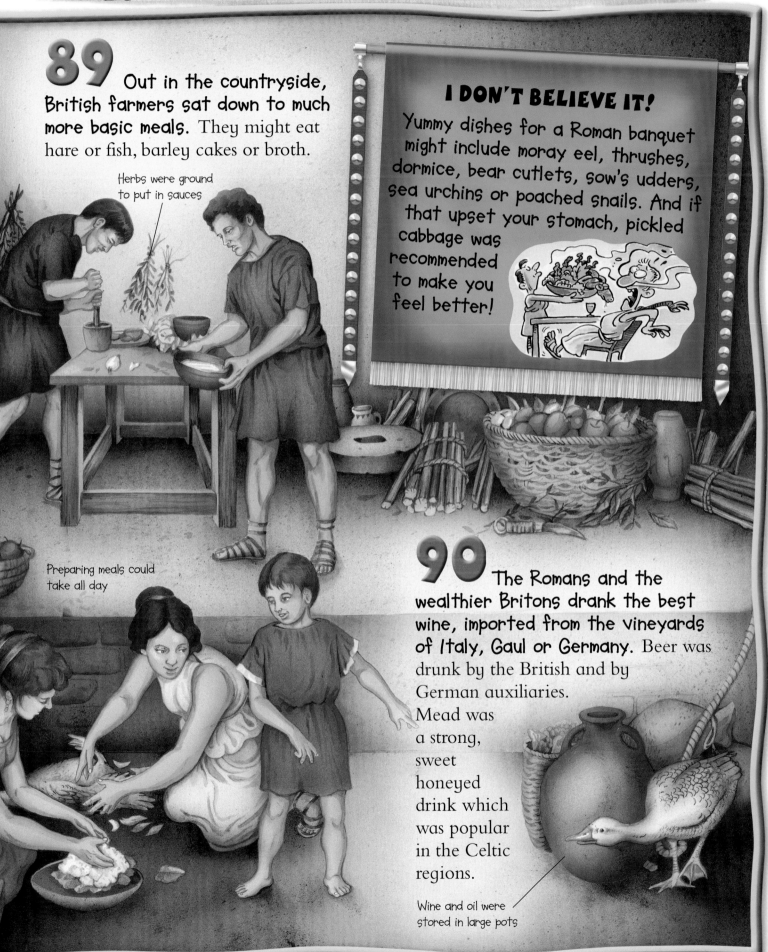

Herbs were ground to put in sauces

Preparing meals could take all day

I DON'T BELIEVE IT!

Yummy dishes for a Roman banquet might include moray eel, thrushes, dormice, bear cutlets, sow's udders, sea urchins or poached snails. And if that upset your stomach, pickled cabbage was recommended to make you feel better!

90 The Romans and the wealthier Britons drank the best wine, imported from the vineyards of Italy, Gaul or Germany. Beer was drunk by the British and by German auxiliaries. Mead was a strong, sweet honeyed drink which was popular in the Celtic regions.

Wine and oil were stored in large pots

A new faith

91 By the AD200s yet another foreign religion was attracting followers in Britannia. It was called Christianity. Christians believed that Jesus Christ, born in a part of the Roman empire called Judaea, was the son of God. They taught that he had been killed on Roman orders but had then arisen from the dead and gone to heaven.

▼ The face of Jesus is shown on this floor mosaic from Dorset. The symbol XP (behind the head) is Greek, standing for chi and rho, the first two letters of the name of Christ.

92 At first the Romans punished the Christians for believing that their God was more powerful than the emperor. Even so, the new faith spread quickly, first among the Britons and then the Romans, rich and poor alike.

◄ One Romanized Briton called Alban was executed in Verulamium in AD209 because he had helped a Christian priest. He was later made a saint and the town was given his name, St Albans.

93
The emperor Constantine made Christianity legal and in AD324 it became the official religion of the empire. Worship of the old gods was still practised in the countryside.

◀ Constantine, son of emperor Constantius, addressing troops in York. In AD306 the legions serving in York proclaimed their backing for Constantine, who had been a successful soldier. He succeeded his father as emperor and became known as Constantine the Great.

94
We know that Christianity spread quickly through Britain in the 300s. There are Christian burial grounds and chapels. Silver chalices have been found, the cups from which Christians drink wine as part of their worship. Lead tanks have been discovered too, which held the water in which new Christians were baptized.

Silver plaque

Silver chalice

QUIZ
Christian bishops were appointed in these Roman towns. Can you unscramble the letters to discover their modern-day names?

1. KORY
2. NOLNOD
3. LOCLINN
4. LESILARC

Answers:
1. York 2. London
3. Lincoln 4. Carlisle

Last of the legions

95 In the later years of the Roman empire, there was division and rebellion in Britannia. In AD286 the empire was divided into an eastern and a western half. In AD287 a Roman admiral called Carausius declared himself ruler of Britain. He was murdered six years later. In AD383 Magnus Maximus, commander of the Roman troops in Britain, marched on Rome and won the throne for five years.

▼ The Saxons from Germany and the Picts from Scotland were just some of the people who tried to invade Britannia as Roman power declined.

Pictish warrior

◄ Britannia was attacked by invaders who sailed across the North Sea.

96 Raiders from outside the empire were circling Britannia like vultures. They wanted to test the strength of their old enemy. Saxons from Germany attacked in the east and south. The Picts were restless in the northeast of Scotland. The Gaels of Ireland (known to the Romans as Scoti) were raiding from the west.

97 In such dangerous times many villa owners buried their money and precious things in secret places, in case of attack by robbers. Some of these treasure hoards have been discovered in modern times.

Saxon settler   Saxon war chief

99 Many Britons by now considered themselves to be Romans and Christians.

But they had to stand on their own. They divided the old province of Britannia into a number of small kingdoms. For hundreds of years these lost land to the invading Angles and Saxons (the ancestors of the English) and to the Gaels (the ancestors of the Highland Scots). The Britons (ancestors of the Welsh and Cornish) were finally cut off in Wales and the west.

98 The Romans were in even bigger trouble on mainland Europe.

Germanic warriors were crossing the river Rhine and flooding into Gaul. From AD401 legions were pulled out of Britannia to meet the threat. In 446 the Britons appealed to Rome to save them, but no help came. In 476 Rome itself fell to a Germanic army. The mighty Roman empire had come to an end.

100 Rome had ruled Britain for nearly 400 years.

It had changed the history of the island for ever, with its language, its law, its towns and roads, its technology and its religion. Rome was never forgotten.

▶ Small Romano-British forces were formed to fight the Saxon raiders. Out of the ruins of Britannia three new lands would emerge – England, Scotland and Wales.

▶ Part of a fine hoard of Roman treasure discovered at Mildenhall, Suffolk, in the 1940s. It included silver spoons, plates, dishes and goblets.

Index